# CONTENTS

Produced by John L. Haag
Printed in the United States of America

Exclusive Distributor for the Entire World:
**CREATIVE CONCEPTS PUBLISHING CORP.**, 2290 Eastman Avenue #110, Ventura, California 93003

# SCHOOL OF RAGTIME

## By SCOTT JOPLIN

REMARKS – What is scurrilously called ragtime is an invention that is here to stay. That is now conceded by all classes of musicians. That all publications masquerading under the name of ragtime are not the genuine article will be better known when these exercises are studied. That real ragtime of the higher class is rather difficult to play is a painful truth which most pianists have discovered. Syncopations are no indication of light or trashy music, and to shy bricks at "hateful ragtime" no longer passes for musical culture. To assist amateur players in giving the "Joplin Rags" that weird and intoxicating effect intended by the composer is the object of this work.

### Exercise No. 1.

It is evident that, by giving each note its proper time and by scrupulously observing the ties, you will get the effect. So many are careless in these respects that we will specify each feature. In this number, strike the first note and hold it through the time belonging to the second note. The upper staff is not syncopated, and is not to be played. The perpendicular dotted lines running from the syncopated note below to the two notes above will show exactly its duration. Play slowly until you catch the swing, and never play ragtime fast at any time.

Slow march tempo (Count Two)

### Exercise No. 2.

This style is rather more difficult, especially for those who are careless with the left hand, and are prone to vamp. The first note should be given the full length of three sixteenths, and no more. The second note is struck in its proper place and the third note is not struck but is joined with the second as though they were one note. This treatment is continued to the end of the exercise.

Slow march tempo (Count Two)

## Exercise No. 3.

This style is very effective when neatly played. If you have observed the object of the dotted lines they will lead you to a proper rendering of this number and you will find it interesting.

Slow march tempo *(Count Two)*

## Exercise No. 4.

The fourth and fifth notes here form one tone, and also in the middle of the second measure and so to the end. You will observe that it is a syncopation only when the tied notes are on the same degree of the staff. Slurs indicate a legato movement.

Slow march tempo *(Count Two)*

## Exercise No. 5.

The first ragtime effect here is the second note, right hand, but, instead of a tie, it is an eighth note: rather than two sixteenths with tie. In the last part of this measure, the tie is used because the tone is carried across the bar. This is a pretty style and not as difficult as it seems on first trial.

Slow march tempo *(Count Two)*

4

## Exercise No.6.

The instructions given, together with the dotted lines, will enable you to interpret this variety which has very pleasing effects. We wish to say here, that the "Joplin ragtime" is destroyed by careless or imperfect rendering, and very often good players lose the effect entirely, by playing too fast. They are harmonized with the supposition that each note will be played as it is written, as it takes this and also the proper time divisions to complete the sense intended.

Slow march tempo *(Count Two)*

# MAPLE LEAF RAG
## By SCOTT JOPLIN

6

# A BREEZE FROM ALABAMA

(A March and Two-Step)
By SCOTT JOPLIN

Not fast.

# THE CASCADES

## By SCOTT JOPLIN

*Tempo di Marcia.*

# THE EASY WINNERS

**(A Ragtime Two-Step)**
**By SCOTT JOPLIN**

*Introduction.*

*Not fast.*

# ELITE SYNCOPATIONS

**By SCOTT JOPLIN**

Not fast.

22

# THE ENTERTAINER

(A Ragtime Two-Step)
By SCOTT JOPLIN

26

# EUGENIA

**By SCOTT JOPLIN**

# FELICITY RAG

(A Ragtime Two-Step)
By SCOTT JOPLIN
and SCOTT HAYDEN

34

# GLADIOUS RAG

## By SCOTT JOPLIN

Slow march tempo.

# PEACHERINE RAG

## By SCOTT JOPLIN

**Not too fast.**

# PINE APPLE RAG

## By SCOTT JOPLIN

Slow March tempo. ♩ = 100

# RAG-TIME DANCE

(A Stop-Time Two-Step)
By SCOTT JOPLIN

**Not too fast**

NOTICE : To get the desired effect of "Stop Time," the pianist will please <u>Stamp</u> the heel of one foot heavily upon the floor at the word "Stamp." Do not raise the toe from the floor while stamping.

Stamp   Stamp   Stamp   Stamp   Stamp   Stamp   Stamp   Stamp

51

# SOMETHING DOING

(A Ragtime Two-Step)
By SCOTT JOPLIN
and SCOTT HAYDEN

Intro.
Not fast.

# THE STRENUOUS LIFE

**(A Ragtime Two-Step)**
**By SCOTT JOPLIN**

*Not fast.*

# SUGAR CANE

## By SCOTT JOPLIN

# SUN FLOWER SLOW DRAG

(A Ragtime Two-Step)
By SCOTT JOPLIN
and SCOTT HAYDEN

# AMERICAN BEAUTY

By JOSEPH F. LAMB

Slow March Tempo.

84

# BOHEMIA

(A Rag)

By JOSEPH F. LAMB

Not fast. ♩ = 100

TRIO

# CHAMPAGNE RAG

(A March and Two-Step)
By JOSEPH F. LAMB

Not fast.

TRIO.

# ETHIOPIA RAG

**By JOSEPH F. LAMB**

Slow March Tempo. ♩= 100.

# RAGTIME NIGHTINGALE

## By JOSEPH F. LAMB

# AMERICAN BEAUTY

## By JOSEPH F. LAMB

Slow March Tempo.

# BOHEMIA

(A Rag)

By JOSEPH F. LAMB

Not fast. ♩ = 100

TRIO

# CHAMPAGNE RAG

(A March and Two-Step)
By JOSEPH F. LAMB

Not fast.

TRIO.

# ETHIOPIA RAG

**By JOSEPH F. LAMB**

Slow March Tempo. ♩ = 100.

# RAGTIME NIGHTINGALE

By JOSEPH F. LAMB

Slow March Tempo.

# REINDEER RAG

**(A Ragtime Two-Step)**
**By JOSEPH F. LAMB**

Not fast. ♩ = 100.

TRIO.

*mp-f* legato.

# PATRICIA RAG

**By JOSEPH F. LAMB**

Slow March Tempo

# EXCELSIOR RAG

## By JOSEPH F. LAMB

Slow March Tempo.

# BROADWAY RAG

## By JAMES SCOTT

# DON'T JAZZ ME-RAG

(I'm Music)

**By JAMES SCOTT**

Not too fast

114

# GREAT SCOTT RAG

**By JAMES SCOTT**

# EVERGREEN RAG

**By JAMES SCOTT**

TRIO.

# THE FASCINATOR

(A March and Two-Step)
By JAMES SCOTT

Not too fast.

# FROG LEGS RAG

**By JAMES SCOTT**

**Not fast.**

# HILARITY RAG

**By JAMES SCOTT**

# ON THE PIKE

(A Ragtime Two-Step)
By JAMES SCOTT

Not too fast.

# OPHELIA RAG

**By JAMES SCOTT**

TRIO.

# THE PRINCESS RAG

**By JAMES SCOTT**

**Not too fast.**

# THE RAGTIME "BETTY"

**By JAMES SCOTT**

# RAGTIME ORIOLE

**By JAMES SCOTT**

*Do not play this piece fast.*

# A SUMMER BREEZE

(A March and Two-Step)
By JAMES SCOTT

* If the octaves are too difficult play the lower notes.

# SUNBURST RAG

**By JAMES SCOTT**

**Not fast.**

155

TRIO.

# KANSAS CITY RAG

**By JAMES SCOTT**

Not too fast.

TRIO.

D.S. 𝄋 al Fine.